LOVE

For
teens

WINS

This book is for every single teenager
out there who has looked around at this
big, broken, beautiful, exotic, troubled,
mysterious, surprising world we live in and
asked, "What am I doing here?"

Love Wins: For Teens
Copyright © 2013 by Rob Bell
All rights reserved. Printed in the United States of America.
No part of this book may be used or reproduced in any manner whatsoever without written permission
except in the case of brief quotations embodied in critical articles and reviews. For information address
HarperCollins Children's Books, a division of HarperCollins Publishers, 10 East 53rd Street, New York,
NY 10022.
www.epicreads.com

Library of Congress Cataloging-in-Publication Data is available.
ISBN 978-0-06-222187-2 (trade bdg.) — ISBN 978-0-06-224844-2 (int'l edition)

Typography by Tom Starace
13 14 15 16 17   LP/RRDH   10 9 8 7 6 5 4 3 2 1
❖
First Edition

LOVE
For teens
WINS

BY ROB BELL

HARPER

An Imprint of HarperCollinsPublishers

CONTENTS

INTRODUCTION
BIKES AND BUTTS

I remember exactly how it felt: It felt like my butt cheek was on fire.

It felt like I wouldn't be able to sit down for days.

Why did I choose to ride the bike and not to shoot the gun?

I have no idea. Seriously, to this day, I have no idea why I chose to ride the bike and not to shoot the gun—but when I was with Brad, I often found myself doing strange things.

Let me explain.

When I was a teenager, I had a crazy friend named Brad.

The crazy friend is the one who doesn't know when to stop, who always takes things too far, who pushes and pushes until:
(a) something breaks
or
(b) somebody gets hurt
or
(c) someone calls the police.

(And everybody has a crazy friend, right? Maybe you even are that friend! Quick test: When you and your friends are out and you toilet-paper someone's house really well and you're hiding in the bushes across the street, admiring your work, is your first impulse afterward to go home and chill out or to go toilet-paper *another* house? If you answered "go toilet-paper another house," then you are, officially, the crazy friend.)

So one day Brad and I were out behind his house, shooting BB guns at targets and bottles and cans. (See, you can already tell this isn't going to end well.)

We did that until we got bored. So we invented a game. We were into BMX bikes at the time, and we invented a game to determine who was the fastest bike rider *and* who could cock the BB gun faster. The game went like this: We'd yell *GO!* and then one of us would jump on the bike and start riding as fast as he could away from the other person, who was furiously cocking the gun so that he could shoot the one on the bike.

I, of course, volunteered to ride the bike, assuming I could ride much faster than Brad could pump the gun and could easily get myself way out of range of his BB gun. Which didn't happen.

As it turns out, he was not only fast but also incredibly accurate.

Getting shot stung like crazy and left a painful welt on my butt cheek. It really hurt. It made it hard to sit down. But it's not like I could tell anybody. Because then I'd have to explain what I did—and that would almost certainly involve describing the game, and that would make me look . . . Well, it'd make me look like an idiot.

Why did Brad and I do things like this all the time?
I have no idea.
The best answer I can think of is: *Because we could*.

Do you know what I mean?
Do you find yourself doing something, and if
someone asked you why, you wouldn't be able to
explain it other than to say something about how you
just felt like it?

One night my friend Kris and I were driving around.
We passed the local grocery store, and Kris said,
"Watch this." She turned into the parking lot, parked
the car, and waited for someone to come out with
their groceries, load up their car, and drive away.
Then she followed them: out of the parking lot,
through the stoplight, down the street. When they
turned, we turned. When they sped up, we sped up.

I sat there in the front seat, laughing so hard I could
barely breathe, before freaking out a mile or so from
the grocery store when it became clear that the other
driver realized they were being followed.

Kris just kept driving.

When I asked her repeatedly why we were following this complete stranger home from the grocery store on a Friday night, she answered, "Because I've always wanted to know what it was like to follow someone." As if it was the most normal thing imaginable.

And that's the thing about it—I remember countless times as a teenager when I did things simply because I wanted to find out what it was like.

Jump off the roof of the house? Did it.
Drive a boat full speed toward the beach and then turn the engine off at the last second so the entire boat went up on the sand? Did it.
Launch bottle rockets from my hand and try to hit my friends with them? Did it.

There's this desire to find out what happens when you do certain things, to discover how people will respond and what it will feel like, and to learn whether or not it will hurt or be funny or be humiliating.

The reason I remember all these pranks and still laugh about them is because they were so different from the rest of life, which had so much pressure—pressure to get good grades and perform and work and achieve and measure up to the standards of the people around me. *Pressure to figure life out.* But the truth was, I was just trying to figure out who I was and what it meant to be comfortable in my own skin, and wondering whether I'd ever be something in the world.

And in that wonder, the only thing it seemed that I knew was that there was always somebody better than me.

There was sports. Which meant there was Steve Belloli. My locker at school was right next to Steve's locker (Bell, Belloli . . .). Every day between classes I would see Steve, and we would talk about classes and sports and girls and all that. I'll never forget the day he told me that he was going to be playing in the football game that Friday night.

What? Football?

Steve and I were on the *soccer* team. What was he doing kicking for the *football* team, let alone the varsity team that played on Friday night? We were *freshmen*. Freshmen didn't play varsity. They just didn't—except, it seemed, for Steve.

As it turns out, the kicker for the varsity team had been crap for the first few games. So the coach had held a tryout and Steve went, even though he'd never kicked field goals, and he beat out everybody for the position. And so that Friday night, as a freshman, he suited up and went out and kicked field goals and kickoffs as if it was the most normal thing ever. And even then, he did it better than anyone could have imagined. On one of his first kickoffs, the kick returner ran through our defense on the return. He only had to beat Steve to score a touchdown.

And what did Steve do?

He tackled the runner. Absolutely leveled the guy. Steve brought him down with such force that people in the stands gasped.

So why do I tell you about Steve Belloli? Because whatever I did, Steve Belloli could do it better. Soccer? Basketball? Football? Steve even went out for tennis, a sport he decided to try at the last minute. I tried out and didn't make the team. Steve tried out

on a whim, made it, and became one of the best
players on the team.

And every day,
between every class,
there he was at his locker,
the one next to mine,
a living, breathing reminder that no matter how
hard I worked and how many practices I went to, he
would always be better than me at sports. And he'd
do it effortlessly in the process. And he'd be nice
about it.

But it wasn't just sports.

My friend Nick was a musician. He'd been playing all
sorts of instruments since he was young, and giving
recitals, and studying classical music. One time I
tried to impress him by playing a song on the piano
that I'd been practicing for months. He listened for
a moment and then asked me when I was going to
be done doing scales. (You know what scales are?
They're what you play when you're warming up to
play an actual song.) Nick honestly thought that the
song I had been working on for countless hours was
just me warming up to play something else.

Ouch.

And then there were grades. My friend Yuko and I had a bunch of classes together, and so sometimes we'd study together. No matter how hard I studied and how much I read, she was always more prepared. It sometimes felt like there was a secret that all the smart people were in on; no matter how much effort I gave, they were always a step ahead.

That's how it always was.
Whatever I did,
there was always someone better.

Have you ever felt like that? Like you can't find *your* thing?
Like everybody else has the thing they're good at, the thing they do, the thing that's theirs, and you don't?
And if you just found that thing you're best at, then everything else would fall into place?

That was me.
Never the best,
with a welt on my butt cheek.

Now I tell you those stories about those people

because there was something else going on in me, something that's still going on with me to this day. My parents are Christians, and growing up, I had heard about Jesus. I listened to stories from them and at church about how Jesus ate with tax collectors and prostitutes, who he wasn't supposed to eat with, how he touched the lepers, who no one else would touch, and how instead of giving people simplistic answers, he often responded to questions by asking more questions. Jesus told offensive, shocking stories about how God loves everybody exactly as we are.

What I picked up from all those stories was that God accepts us whether we're winners or losers, good or bad, cool or insanely dorky, whether we are king or queen of our school or if every day is a struggle just to get out of bed in the morning.

This message was a big deal to me then, because the world I lived in *was all about* ranking and competing and deciding who were the winners and who were the losers.

But Jesus didn't measure my worth by what I had won or accomplished or achieved or who I was better than. And that idea blew my mind.

I remember there was a huge party that it seemed like everybody was invited to, but I wasn't. When I asked a kid why, he said, "Because you're not popular," as if it was obvious. I replayed that line, "Because you're not popular," over and over in my head for days. And yet I'd hear stories about Jesus in which he seemed to say that there was another way to see life, a way that didn't care about someone's system of who's popular and who's not.

But it wasn't just that Jesus insisted that God loves us exactly as we are. The message I also picked up over time was that Jesus had something for me to do in the world. I was meant to lead a meaningful life in which I could do something that would matter, something that would make the world a better place.

This message had a powerful effect on me. There still were my everyday struggles and doubts and humiliations—

I remember riding the bench on the soccer team one year, and in a particular game, I didn't get in at all. At the end my uniform was perfectly clean, while most of the other players' uniforms were dirty—

I remember getting caught cheating on an exam.
The teacher stood up from his desk and walked
slowly across the room to my desk and picked up
my test and wrote a big, red *F* on it and then put it
back down on my desk and walked slowly back to his
chair, with everybody watching and knowing exactly
what was going on.

(I was actually giving answers to a kid who hadn't
studied. Who gets caught cheating not because they
don't have the answers but because they do? How
lame is that?)

I remember there was a girl who lived on the other
side of the neighborhood, who I asked out several
times. She kept saying no, but it wasn't until she told
me that she couldn't because she was doing laundry
with her sisters that I realized she had no interest in
going out with me.

There were those struggles and embarrassments and
failures. There were all the times I didn't get invited
to the parties that the popular kids were throwing.
But then at the same time I had this sense that there

was another standard, another system, another way of seeing the world—and in that way of seeing things, I was in some way going to be okay.

It's really hard to explain (and will take most of this book!), but at some level through all that confusion and pressure and doubt and humiliation, I had a sense that my life mattered and that I was loved and that there was something for me to do in the world and that I would eventually figure it out.

I had faith,
and that made a huge difference.

So that's what this book is about:
It's about faith,
the kind that gives you hope about yourself,
hope about your future,
and hope about the world we live in.

Now, before we get started, let me pause here and say a few things about faith, because in the following pages I'll talk about God and Jesus and the Bible and grace and love and heaven and hell and all sorts of things that are usually brought up when people are talking about religion.

You've probably heard many different ideas from different people about these issues. It can all be a bit overwhelming, a bit maddening, and sometimes incredibly discouraging. It's hard to know who to trust and who is full of rubbish and who has other agendas.

So let me say this: Any faith that doesn't give you lots of room to question and search and discover for yourself isn't a faith worth having.

My hope and prayer for this book is that it helps you find the freedom to ask questions, to explore, to push back, to imagine and discuss—and to sort it out for yourself. I want to help you on your way as you wrestle with the questions in your life. Questions have a funny way of taking us places we didn't expect and showing us all sorts of possibilities. I think of my friends Lizzie and Anthony and Brandon and Jane, who are all teenagers who have had all sorts of questions about their faith. They didn't bury them or avoid them. They asked them honestly and pursued answers and studied other perspectives than the ones they'd grown up with. My friend Joey grew up in church, but the messages he heard didn't make sense. He felt like there was something more, there had to be something more, so he went on a search of sorts, reading all kinds of religious books and going to a variety of different kinds of services from a variety of different traditions. I just saw him recently, and he's thriving—he has a deep, real connection with God. And one of the reasons he's doing so well is that he wasn't content to just swallow what he was fed, but he took ownership of his faith.

Which leads me to a quick thought about spiritual leaders, pastors, rabbis, teachers, and ministers: Any spiritual leader who doesn't encourage you in your desire to search and explore and question *so that* you can own your faith for yourself is not someone who should be followed.

My desire is that this book helps you find the freedom to search and discover and think and believe for yourself. In the process, I know you'll find what you're looking for: the full, vibrant, overflowing, creative, surprising life that Jesus insists we can have right now.

Ready?
Let's get started.

CHAPTER 1
EVERYONE IS INVITED

I remember sitting in the visiting room of a mental hospital, talking with a teenager I'd known for years who had just had a breakdown. His life had spun out of control and he felt like he was losing his mind, and so his parents checked him into this treatment center. We talked for a while about his life and his problems and his anxiety and depression, but what was so strange was that he kept bringing up his brother—how amazing and smart and talented his older brother was—and that he could never measure up.

It was almost—and I'm trying to find the best way to say this—it was like *he wished he was his brother*.

It seemed like somewhere along the way, he had bought into the idea that he would never be as good as his brother. Like he believed that he was doomed to live in his shadow.

I know this sounds like an issue between him and his brother, but sitting there in that mental hospital, I started to wonder if his real issue wasn't actually with God. My friend didn't like who God made when God made him. Now I realize you may or may not believe in God, but whether you do or not, we all have beliefs about who we are and why we're here that shape our lives in countless ways.

I tell you about visiting him in that mental hospital because our images of God are crucial for how we understand our lives. Some people believe there's nothing out there, that we're all alone, that there is no God helping us and guiding us, and so that shapes how they see life. Others see God as an angry old man with a long beard who can't wait to judge everybody. And others see God as the one to blame for whatever is wrong in their life—from the shape of their body to their parents' divorce to their brother's successes to the traumas or tragedies they've experienced.

So what I want to do here is give you a way to think about God, which will lead us to a number of questions about who we are and what we're doing here.

So here's the idea, the idea that drives this whole book, the idea we'll return to again and again:

God is throwing a party,
and everyone's invited.

Now when I use that word "party," I'm sure you have some images in your head. I remember when I was seventeen and walking in the front door of a house where a girl from my school was throwing a party because her parents were out of town. My friend John was sitting on the couch, and he was really, really drunk, talking really, really loudly, and really, really annoying everybody.

Sound familiar?

Whether it's getting wasted
or blitzed
or lit

or trashed

or sloshed

or tanked

or schlitzed

or plastered

or hammered

or lubed

or baked

or cooked

or whatever it is—I'm sure you and your friends have your own words for it!—for many people, when they say *party*, what they mean is *escape*. Escape from pressure, school, parents, work, authority, rules— and we all know that that often involves drinking or smoking or taking something to get their minds off . . . well . . . *life*.

So there's that understanding of party.

But it's not the only one. There's another understanding of the word "party" that comes from the ancient world of the Bible. Do you know how the Bible ends? With God living with people in peace. The writer describes the scene like a wedding banquet, which would have been like a party that went on for days and days, with food and dancing and stories and music. In the ancient world, they threw epic parties. The events took months of planning and often took people days to walk to and sometimes cost a lot of money, all to celebrate the fact that for once, for now, life is good.

"Good" is even one of the first words in the Bible, and it refers to what God wants for us: God's desire for us to thrive here on earth, to enjoy our lives and our work and our friends, to care for the earth, and to live in peace with everything and everybody.

I realize that's a big sentence, but it's the big idea that's in the Bible over and over and over again. It's not that there won't be suffering or heartache or pain or death—we'll talk more about that in a moment— but the central story is about God's desire for us to live in God's good world in God's way.

Do you know what this means?
God is for us.
God is for *you*.

I know this is really basic, but it's incredibly important to understanding faith that we're clear from the beginning that God is for you. I was talking to this guy who had just gotten out of high school. He'd gotten a girl pregnant, and he was angry that this had happened. He told me at one point, "I just can't get a break!" as if God was somehow against him. I've actually met tons of people like him, who over the years have come to believe for some reason or another that God is against them. I can't tell you how many people I've met who won't go to a church service because they're sure the roof will cave in or that they'll get hit by lightning bolts. Now, we laugh at the idea of the roof actually collapsing or a random lightning bolt hitting someone in broad daylight just because they walked through the door of a church, but underneath it all what they're saying is that their image of God is of a divine being who is just waiting to punish them. I think of a high school girl I know who believes that she's worthless and that when God made her, God made a mistake.

The God that Jesus talked about is *for her*.
And you.

Do you believe that?
That God is *for you*?
Jesus had this great line about how God causes it to rain on good people and bad people. That was

significant in Jesus' day, because rain was how crops grew, which was how people got their food. To say that God gives rain to everybody was to say that God is *for everybody*.

So whatever you're going through,
whether you struggle in school
or you have a relative with cancer
or you have secrets you haven't shared with anybody
or you keep hooking up with people and then regretting it,
God is for you.

When God made you, God did not make a mistake.

Now, on to the next big idea: I believe not only that God is for you, but Jesus came to bring us God's love and forgiveness and grace, because we all need it. I got a call a few years ago from a high school student who was pregnant, and her boyfriend was doing drugs, and she was terrified. It was a massive mess, and for her, the worst part was her own sense of guilt and shame.

We can easily become haunted by the things we've done, can't we? Mistakes, sins, things we wish no one knew about, things we've kept hidden. Sometimes it can feel like our past is following us everywhere we go, can't it?

Jesus' message was about the grace of God, forgiving us and cleaning us up and washing us and leaving the past where it belongs—in the past. This is why the cross is so important to Jesus' message. He never stops insisting that all the ways we've blown it and screwed up and sinned and fallen short and missed the mark have been taken care of by him on the cross. He even said at one point that he didn't come to condemn, he came to save us. One of the first Christians wrote that in Jesus we're *new creations*. That means that the old goes away and something new, something good comes into our lives. I met this fourteen-year-old kid named Shane years ago, who was seriously addicted to drugs. The more we talked, the more he insisted that there wasn't really any hope for him.

If you could have seen the look on his face—let alone the look on his mother's face—it was so incredibly sad. Eventually he was sent to a really intense boot camp program for addicts, and guess what? It worked. It actually worked. He cleaned up and came

home and finished school and then got a job. I didn't
see him until years later, and when he walked up
to me, I knew I'd met this young man before, but I
couldn't place him. When he said his name, I about
fell over—*Are you kidding me?* You're that kid who was
in so deep years ago? And now you're standing here
healthy and clean? Amazing.

So when I read that passage in the Bible about
someone becoming a new creation in Jesus, I've seen
that up close with my own eyes.

Do you believe this?
Do you trust that when Jesus said on the cross, "It is
finished," he was talking about you and me and all
our junk and garbage and regrets and mistakes and
sins?

Let me take a minute here to say a few quick things
about religion, okay? It's really important we're
clear that the one thing faith—honest, true, real
faith—does more than anything is it humbles us. We
realize that God has given us a gift, and over time we
become more and more grateful. This is incredibly
important when you're growing up and there are all
these authority figures around you who each, in their

own way, insist that they're right and you should do things their way.

Have you ever been told that things were a certain way by someone and you couldn't decide whether to trust them or not? Here's one way to help you decide who to listen to and who not to: Is this person humbled by the gift God has given them? Real, true, honest faith will always lead to humility. You'll sense it in everything they do. When I was fifteen, I became friends with a youth leader named Ray, who was in his twenties. When he was younger, he'd gotten caught up in dealing drugs and doing all sorts of illegal stuff. But then he had a genuine rebirth experience, where he encountered the love and grace and peace of Jesus. He straightened up and decided to help out with a youth group by organizing the sports so he could tell kids like me his story. The thing that was so inspiring about him was that he was humble. He never tried to push his faith on anyone. He had this love of life and this gratitude that flowed out of him—and you couldn't help but ask him questions about how he found the happiness he had.

Remember the teenager I visited in the mental

hospital? I saw him several months after he'd gotten out, and he looked like a different person. He explained that while he was in the hospital, he'd realized how much of his life had been dominated by guilt and shame and blaming God for who he wasn't—namely his brother—and he realized that wasn't any way to live. He went through a process of turning it over to Jesus and leaving it there on the cross, where it belongs. The result was a startling transformation.

He found the unconditional love that Jesus says is ours. It humbled him. You could see it on his face before he ever said a word.

God is for us.
God offers us grace and forgiveness in Jesus.
God loves us exactly as we are.

Now, more about the party. I purposely used the words "God" and "party" in the same sentence, because I know for a lot of people, when they hear the word "God," the last thing that comes to mind is a *party*. For many, the word "God" brings to mind rules and commands and debates and religions—God can seem like the guy who kills the party, who calls the cops, who turns off the music, the buzzkill who shuts the party down.

But Jesus gives us a different image of God and the life God has for us. And to talk about that, we're going to need to talk about heaven. . . .

CHAPTER 2
HEAVEN

When I was a kid, my grandmother had this painting over the couch in her living room.

As you can see, in the center of the picture is a massive cross, big enough for people to walk on. It hangs suspended in space, floating above a frightening red-and-black realm that threatens to swallow whoever takes a wrong step. The people in the picture walking on the cross are clearly headed somewhere—and that somewhere is a city. A gleaming, bright city with a wall around it and lots of sunshine.

I show you this painting because it tells a story.

It's a story about people moving from one place to another with the bridge as the way from the one place to the other place. The idea behind the painting is that the people are going to heaven, which means they have to walk over the endless scary pit. But it also tells another story: According to the painting, all of this is happening somewhere else.

Giant crosses do not hang suspended in the air in the world that you and I call home! Cities don't float. And if you tripped and fell off the cross/sidewalk in this world, you would not free-fall indefinitely down into an abyss of giant red caves and hissing steam.

I show you this painting because, as surreal as it is, the fundamental story that it tells about heaven— that it is somewhere else—is the story that many people know to be the Christian story. When I was in high school, I went to a church service, and the preacher said that the reason Jesus came was so that we could go to heaven someday.

I remember thinking, *That's the best Jesus can do? Give me hope about something that might happen someday, somewhere else?*

Think of the images that are associated with heaven: harps and clouds and streets of gold, everybody dressed in a white robe. (Does anybody look good in a white robe? Can you play sports in a white robe? How could it be heaven without sports? What about swimming? What if you spill food on it?)

Think of all the jokes that begin with someone showing up at the gates of heaven and Saint Peter is there, like a bouncer at a club, deciding who does and doesn't get to go behind the velvet rope.

Most people in our world seem to think of heaven first and foremost as somewhere else, sometime else. This is why so many teenagers can easily find church so boring: If the basic message is how to get somewhere else when you die, what does that have to do with grades and growing up and boyfriends and girlfriends and parents who don't understand?

No wonder religion can seem so irrelevant.

And so the questions that are asked about heaven often have an otherworldly air to them:
What will we do all day?
Will we recognize people we used to know?

What will it be like?
Will there be dogs there?

I've heard pastors answer, "It will be unlike anything
we can comprehend, like a church service that goes
on forever," to which some think, *That sounds more
like hell!*

Now, I write all this about heaven because I want
you to see how Jesus talked about heaven, because
for Jesus, heaven wasn't some far-off place that was
only relevant when you die; he saw the life of heaven
as a kind of life we can enter into now. It's as if he
kept saying, "The party's already started! You don't
have to wait!"

That's my hope for you,
that you discover this kind of life.

To get at what this life looks like, I'm going to need to
give you a little background. So hang with me. We're
going to cover some ground in the Bible so that we
better understand Jesus' message, and then we'll
spend quite a bit of time applying all this to the very
practical questions of our everyday lives.

Sound good?

First, we all realize that the world we live in is really, really messed up, right? From divorce to kids cutting themselves to pollution to bullying to younger and younger teens using drugs, we all know that something is not right with the world. I will never forget getting the call that my friend Gordie from high school had killed himself. I just sat there in shock for a while, trying to understand something that I'll never understand.

Ever had that feeling?
Ever asked this question: Is it always going to be like this?
Or this question: Is the world ever going to get better?
Or how about this one: Is hope real?

Me too.

People have had these questions for thousands of years, because people have longed for the world to be fixed, made right, restored, cleansed—however you describe it, there's been a desire deep in the bones of humanity since the beginning for the world to be as it's supposed to be. My friend Dave was sixteen when two men broke into his neighbor's house early in the morning to rob it. As they were leaving the house, Dave's mom was walking out to the street to get the newspaper and saw them. One of them pulled out a gun and shot her, right there in her front yard. Dave's dad then had to wake him and his brothers and sisters up to tell them that their mom had just died. I hung out with Dave for the next several days, driving around, listening to music, talking, trying to make sense of it all, overwhelmed with grief. I'm sure you've had those moments as well, moments and events and experiences that filled you with a deep-seated sense that this is not how it's supposed to be.

Now, I want you to see how Jesus answered these questions, because it will help us understand what faith can look like in our modern world.

Jesus came from a Jewish tradition that had faith that there would be answers to those questions: They believed that God hadn't deserted or abandoned the world but that God was at work in human history, and God was going to do something massive in the future to heal the world. They believed that God had plans to restore the world to the way God always intended it to be.

The prophet Isaiah (who lived several hundred years before Jesus) said the earth would be
"filled with the knowledge of God"
and there would be
"a feast of rich food for all peoples."

(See how when the prophet here speaks of what God was going to do in the future, he uses an image people would have been familiar with: a party!)

Now, to make sure we're clear how they understood this future day, let me ask you a question: Have you ever been sitting in class and someone in the back of the room was screwing around and distracting you so you couldn't hear the teacher? It's totally annoying and you just wish the teacher would tell them to stop?

You wanted the teacher to act,
to do something decisive,
to shut that kid up, right?

That's what Jesus and his tradition believed God was going to do in the future with anything that got in the way of people flourishing in God's good world. They believed that God was going act decisively to put an end to war and violence and gossip and racism and famine and rape and everything else you can think of that is not right with the world.

And so they spoke of a cleansing, purging, decisive day when God would make things right. They called this day the "Day of the Lord." The day when God says "ENOUGH!" to anything that threatens the peace and harmony and health that God intends for the world.

This would be a day when a number of things that can survive in the world now would no longer be able to survive in the world.

Have you ever gotten really angry when you saw something wrong, like a bully pushing around someone younger or weaker, and everything within you said, *Somebody needs to do something about that!!!!*

You in that moment were longing for justice, for the world to be restored and made right.

And so that is the promise of the prophets who came

before Jesus: that someday God would act decisively
on behalf of everybody who's ever been stepped on,
lied about, abused, ignored, hurt, mistreated, robbed,
forgotten, or mistreated.

God would put an end to it.
God would say, "Enough!!"

Now I've given you just a little background in the
tradition Jesus came from, but do you notice where
they believed all this was going to take place?

Here.
Earth.
Our home.

In the Bible, when they talked about where we would
all be someday, they talked about this world being
fixed and healed and transformed into the place God
had intended it to be all along.

Not somewhere else,
here.

(By the way, the idea of taking care of the earth and
using less electricity and recycling and keeping our

beaches and parks and streets free from litter—
that's at the very heart of the Christian faith. We only
get one home. . . .)

So there's a bit of background about how Jesus and
his tradition thought about the future. Now, one more
bit of background: For Jesus, the place where things
are how God wants them to be is called heaven.

Here on earth we can do whatever we want. We can
lie or cheat or steal or do anything destructive we
want, right? We can also choose to do good, to be
generous, kind, honest, and positive.

There's heaven,
where things are as God wants them to be,
and then there's earth,
where things are lots of different ways:
some good, some really, really bad.

So when Jesus anticipated that great day in the
future when God would heal the world, he was talking
about the day when heaven and earth *would be the
same place*.

This is really, really important, so let me repeat it:

When Jesus spoke of the future, he spoke about the coming day when heaven and earth would be one.

For Jesus, heaven is a real part of God's creation—a part that we can't access at this time. His belief was that at some point that part would come here and be united with the rest of God's creation, with earth.

Got that?
Because it's a big idea,
and it's one that has huge implications for the lives we live,
especially when you're a teenager and you're trying to figure out what you're going to do with your life.

One more big idea,
then we'll get really practical with all this.

When Jesus talked about what God was going to do someday in fixing and restoring and healing the world, he insisted that God was beginning this great new work through him.

So when Jesus healed someone, he did it to show that God's new world had already begun through him.

And when he provided food for masses of hungry people, he did it to show that he was beginning the great work of redeeming the world.

And when he died on the cross and then rose from the dead, the first Christians saw this as the first act of the new creation of the world.

Imagine there's this junior in high school and he's been dating this girl who's a sophomore for a year and prom is coming and he's thinking about asking her to go with him. What does he do?

He sends her a text asking her, right?
Nope.

He calls his friend and asks his friend to go over to her house and ask her to go to prom with him, right?
Nope.

Why not?
Because with something that important, he goes himself. He goes over to her house, they go for a walk or to their favorite coffee place, and then he asks her face-to-face.

Because when it really matters,

you don't send someone else.

This is how the first Christians understood Jesus. They believed that God had come in person in Jesus to invite each and every one of us to be a part of the new world that God is creating.

As time went on, they came up with more and more ways of explaining it, but the central belief they returned to again and again is that all of creation is in trouble, and so God came among us in flesh and blood to take the pain and suffering upon himself. Jesus dying and then rising again three days later was a display for them of God's power to overcome the very worst pain, suffering, and evil anybody could ever experience.

These are huge claims and massive ideas. And Jesus' first disciples never seemed to run out of ways to describe God's power and celebrate it.

Which takes us back again to the party.

Jesus told a number of stories about people throwing parties and inviting all sorts of unexpected people, because he wanted people to know that God's new life is for all of us. God doesn't show any favoritism, because God wants us all to live with God in the new world God is making.

Jesus even had a way of talking about this new life: He called it eternal life, because it was an endless life lived at peace with God. Jesus repeatedly said that he came to give us this new kind of life—one that was overflowing and creative and vibrant and real.

Now, it may seem like all this was a new idea, but it actually goes way back to the beginning. This understanding of heaven ultimately being *here* was not a new idea in Jesus's day. It came from the earliest scriptures. In the first book of the Bible, Genesis, people are turned loose in a garden to name the animals and care for the earth and enjoy it. That's actually the second command in the Bible: to take care of the earth. To name is to order, to participate, to partner with God in taking the world somewhere.

If we were to summarize the beginning of the Bible, it's as if God says:
"Here it is, a big, beautiful, fascinating world. Do

something with it!"

Jesus lived with an awareness that God has been looking for partners since the beginning, people who jump in and live life to the fullest and do something with this big, beautiful, mysterious world.

Have you ever been hiking in the mountains or swimming in the ocean or walking through a forest and found the beauty of it overwhelming?

Of course, it's actually written in the Bible that that's one of the ways we encounter God, through creation.

Have you ever made something—built something around the house, written a poem, done something in art class—and found it incredibly satisfying?

Of course, because God is the creator, and God created us to be creators.

Have you ever helped someone who needed it—from yard work to visiting them in the hospital to taking them a meal to shoveling the snow off their driveway—and been amazed at how meaningful it was?

Of course, because you were doing your part to make the world a better place.

God gives us life and turns us loose to do something with it!

So when you start living how God intends for us to live, you're living the life of heaven, now.

When Jesus calls disciples,
how does he teach them to pray?
He teaches them to pray to God,
"Your will be done on earth,
as it is in heaven."

Jesus called his disciples—his students of life—to learn from him how to live in God's world God's way, now, bringing heaven to earth.

Wow, that's a lot of background.
Now let's get practical.

First, life is a gift, no matter how hard and grueling

and unfair it appears to be at times.

Do you believe this?

I guarantee that the people you most admire and look up to are people who believe that each day is a gift and thank God for it.

Maybe you have a brother or sister who is a complete pain in the ass, or a particular teacher who you wish would fall over dead, or a coach or parent or neighbor who makes your blood boil—no one get a free pass from the agony of life, do they?

I remember when Hurricane Katrina hit and the Gulf Coast was so devastated. It was so hard to see the pictures of how many people had lost their homes. It's easy to get angry with God or the weather or whatever at times like that, and to wonder why there's so much suffering in the world. But I know a group of middle school students who started raising money to help people who had lost their homes get back on their feet. They made YouTube clips and organized events and spread the word. It was incredible to watch how they responded.

Because the truth is, you have a choice. You have a choice every single day. You can choose to be bitter and cynical and jaded and angry or grateful and generous and loving.

This isn't easy, is it?

There are a lot of reasons to be resentful and feel like you got shafted by life, like you're entitled to more. It's easy to get mad at life for handing out so much pain.

But that kind of thinking will always make us miserable.

The truth about the choices we have every day helps us understand why Jesus called disciples. A disciple is a student of life, someone learning from the master how to live in the best possible way. Jesus even told his disciples to go out and make more disciples, to teach more people how to live the Jesus way.

Jesus calls disciples in order to teach us how to be and what to be—his intention is for us to grow in generosity and forgiveness and honesty and courage

and truth telling and responsibility, so that as these
take over our lives, we are taking part more and more
and more in the life of heaven, now.

You know what this means?
You can take it easy on yourself.
Stop beating yourself up.
Stop worrying that you don't have your act together
right now.

Remember that teen I visited in the mental hospital?
My message to him was: Stop trying to be someone
you're not and start enjoying the person that you are.

Stop stressing that you're not perfect.
Stop distressing over all the questions that you don't
know how to answer.
Stop freaking out about all the people who can do
things better than you can.

God didn't make you to be them.
God made you to be you.

For years as a pastor, I liked to stick around after
the church service to talk with people. I'd often have
conversations with teens who were stressed about

something—usually involving their frustration with themselves.

I think of Jim, a brilliant musician who struggled with his self-worth to the point where he would often spend days thinking about killing himself, imagining how he'd do it. And then he'd sort of snap out of it and feel terrible that he'd been thinking like that. It was like a pattern, a habit, a dark vortex he couldn't seem to get out of. . . .

And Rachel, who felt like she was supposed to have answers for all her friends' questions about religion.

Relax.
When you trust Jesus,
you become one of his students.
You're learning.

Jesus doesn't expect you to have it all figured out,
so you shouldn't either.

We're disciples, learning how to be more patient,
more kind,
more courageous.
Do you ever freeze up in moments when you wish you

had the guts to do something brave and bold?
Do you ever wish you had more of a spine?

Here's what a disciple does: You take that wish and
you turn it into a prayer and you ask Jesus to help
give you more of a spine. If you read the Sermon on
the Mount, which is in the Bible in Matthew, chapters
5–7, what you see really quickly is that Jesus is
giving practical advice on how to deal with the sorts
of challenges and issues that we deal with every day.

How do you forgive somebody who has really hurt
you?
How do you deal with people in your life who are
really controlling?
How do you find the strength not to get revenge when
someone wrongs you?

This is what Jesus does. He comes to teach us how
to live a better way, God's way in God's world.

And it takes time,
and patience,
and most of all, intention.

I have some friends who started a punk band in

high school, and they would come every single Sunday night, as a band, to the church where I was preaching. There'd they'd be; sometimes they'd played a gig the night before, and they'd driven all through the night to get home, but they'd be there. They were so hungry to learn and grow and take it all in. What I found so inspiring about them was their determination to figure out how their faith influenced all the areas of their lives. They instinctively understood that Jesus invites us into a whole way of life, and throwing your energy into being one of his disciples makes all the difference. Even when you're in a punk band.

You may find church boring or irrelevant, but try this: Try going to a service and listening for just one thing that will help you become a better disciple. Listen for just that one thing and then go put it into practice.

Some days you'll make huge progress, and some days you'll feel like you took a step backward.

But what you do is you make the choice that you're going to become a disciple, you're going to start learning, and then you go after it, day after day after day.

This leads me to another truth about faith: It's the small things. Sometimes when you're a teen, it's easy to get the feeling that you're supposed to go out and be an epic hero, the guy or girl who battles the odds and does something that's never been done before.

You know what I'm talking about. We love heroes because they inspire us, but they also can really mess with your mind, can't they?

Ever had that experience?
You hear about a sixteen-year-old girl sailing around the world alone, and it's as if you're being asked the question: So what did you do this summer?

But here's the truth about living the life of heaven right now: It's about doing the next right thing.

It may be volunteering an hour a week.
It may mean befriending the loser who sits in the back of math class.
It may lead you to one kind act that no one will ever see.

I remember when I was growing up and people would talk about this famous preacher named Billy Graham who would preach and a million people would come. The crowd would be so big that from the stage he couldn't see the back of the crowd.

Are you and I ever going to do something like that? Seriously?
Probably not!

Or Mother Teresa? What are the odds that you are going to start a mission to the poor in India?

You may,
or you may not.

So don't worry about how big whatever it is you're going to do with your life is; that's not the point. The point is you trusting that God has something for you to do in the world to make it more and more the place that God intends for it to be.

When I was sixteen, I had the most boring history teacher in . . . history. She was dreadful. She would take these stories from the past about people marching for thousands of miles and exploring new worlds and dying for their causes and giving their lives for their ideals, and she somehow managed to suck the life right out of everything. It got to the point where you just wanted to beat your head against the wall or jump out the window of the classroom.

Awful, just awful.
I'd rather get hit in the head with a rock than go to her class.

But guess what I've learned?

You know what I do for my work now? I tell stories and I write books and I make films. And I work very, very hard to make those stories and books and films interesting so that people will be engaged and inspired.

You see where I'm going with this, right?

Sometimes the things that may frustrate you the most—like a terrible history teacher—are actually God's way of getting your attention, showing you little glimpses of what your work in the world is going to be. Pay close attention to the things that anger you, because somewhere in there may be signs of your future!

I have a friend who hates it when people are phony. He absolutely hates it. It drives him crazy. As a result, he's literally the most honest person you've ever met. He tells you exactly what he's thinking all the time. You know what he does for a job? He goes around speaking to businesses and organizations and schools, teaching people how to communicate more honestly and effectively. And he's really, really good at it.

It started when he was young. He realized that there was a pattern that kept recurring in his life—he'd be talking with people, and he'd cut through the mindless small talk and get right to what people were really thinking and feeling. He had this desire to slice through the bullshit and get right to the real issues, and, wouldn't ya know it, it turned into his life's work.

This is key to being a disciple: You're always paying attention to what's going on inside you, because you live with the conviction that God is with you and for you and has a purpose for you in the world. So you're constantly praying and opening yourself up and asking God to give you eyes to see what the next right thing to do is.

Now, on to more practical truths about you and your role in the world. Jesus talked about seeking God's kingdom. Do that and the rest would fall into place.

Here's what he means: It's easy to get hung up on the specifics and find yourself really disoriented and frustrated. It's easy when you're a teen to get hung up on the details—where you're going to go to college or whether or not you're going to make the team or get a certain teacher next year. And these are incredibly important things that deserve and demand tons of our energy and time.

But when you follow Jesus,
they aren't first.

What's first is you being open to letting God transform you into more and more and more the person you were created to be.

Here's an example: Whether you end up teaching

in a school or running a household or working in government or writing novels or building a business, Jesus' desire is that you are a generous, giving, joyful person wherever you find yourself. If your heart is being shaped in those ways, you'll impact and influence people wherever you are. Those particulars about where you live and who you work with and how successful you are—those will come and go. But the kind of person you're becoming—
that's the deal,
that's the real challenge,
that's what life is really about.

So try lots of things. Ask people you admire if you can follow them around for the day. Volunteer in lots of different organizations. Save up your money and travel as much as you can. When you're with people older than you, ask them tons of questions about where they went to school and what they love to do and what were the hardest things they've ever had to do and what makes them angry and were there ever times when they wanted to give up and what's their idea of a perfect day?

Over time, you'll see that you're drawn to certain things more and more; they'll grab you and draw you in. When I was a sophomore in high school, I was in a government class and our assignment was to give a presentation—which we could do any way we wanted. My friends and I dressed up as characters from *Saturday Night Live* and made a film—which was a blast to make—and we all got As. I wasn't the smartest in the class, but when it came to making something and then sharing it with people, I was right at home.

And what do I do now?
I create things and share them with people.

The seeds of who I've become and what I do now were there years ago.

So what does this have to do with you?

God is for you,
and God has created you with particular talents and gifts and desires—
so pay really careful attention to what you're drawn to, because somewhere in there, you're going to find your true self, the person you were created to be.

And that process of discovering who you are,

it's the most important and exhilarating and thrilling thing imaginable.

Which leads to another big idea about living the life of heaven now: What you believe about the future shapes, informs, and determines how you live now.

If you believe that you're going to leave and evacuate to somewhere else, then why do anything positive in this world? A proper view of heaven leads not to escape from the world, but full engagement with it, all with the anticipation of a coming day when things are on earth as they are in heaven.

This is incredibly important to think about when you're young. At the center of the Bible's vision for life is the affirmation that each of us has a role to play in the world. We all have a way to participate with God in making a better world. I've met teens who have a strong sense deep in their heart of their role, their calling, their path, but they've been discouraged by friends or family or authority figures.

Sometimes they've been told that a person can't make a lot of money doing whatever it is. Sometimes they're called to do something that's

never been done before, and so people simply don't
understand what they're talking about.
And sometimes they're the first in their family to care
about a particular cause or mission or field of study,
and so they get blank stares when they talk about it.

This can all be incredibly discouraging, but you have
to press on and try new things and have faith that if
you're true to who you are and you find wise mentors
who can lead you, it's extraordinary what's possible.

Heaven isn't about escaping this world,
it's about saying yes to Jesus's invitation to work for
a better world.

So, that's a lot, huh?
One more thought to wrap this part of the book up:

Jesus believes in you.

I know that for lots of teens, when they hear the
words "faith" or "religion" or "church" or "Bible,"
the first thing that comes to mind is them believing
in God, because that's often how pastors talk.
You're supposed to believe certain things so you can
have peace with God or so you can go to heaven or

whatever it is.

But there's another way to see it.

The Bible tells the story of a God who believes in people. And that, of course, includes teens. In fact, a lot of people think Jesus's first disciples were probably in their late teens.

And what does Jesus do with them? He tells them to go out and make more disciples, and then he leaves them.

Huh?
He leaves them?

Yes! That's the point!

He leaves them to spread his message without him, because he believes that they can do it. You don't ask somebody to do something and then leave them alone to do it unless you actually think they can.

So when it comes to the life of heaven,
to the kind of life Jesus came to give us,
he believes that you and I can do it.

He trusts that we can be courageous and generous
and loving and kind and creative and innovative and
daring and compassionate and honest. . . .

Don't ever forget that.
Jesus invites you to believe in him,
to trust him,
to follow him,
to accept him as the savior and teacher Christians
have believed he is for two thousand years.
But he also believes in you.
That you can be the kind of person who brings
heaven to earth.

CHAPTER 3
HELL

I remember arriving in Africa in December 2002 and driving from the airport in Kigali, Rwanda, to our hotel. On the way, I saw a kid, probably ten or eleven, standing by the side of the road with a missing hand. Then I saw another, just down the street, missing a leg. Then another in a wheelchair. Hands, arms, legs—I must have seen several hundred teenagers with missing limbs in just those first several miles. My guide explained what had happened during the genocide roughly ten years earlier: The Hutu people came to believe that another group of people, the Tutsi, had to be defeated at all costs and forever. The Hutu decided that the most effective way to degrade and humiliate their enemy was to remove an arm or a leg of a young Tutsi child with a machete. This way that child would have to live forever with the reminder of what was done to him—and anyone who saw him would also know (and come to fear) the power of the Hutu warriors.

I can't begin to tell you how crushing it was to hear that story and see all those kids. It never ceases to amaze me the unspeakable evil that humans are capable of.

I've been a pastor for twenty years, and I've had a front-row seat to all the ways people choose not to take part in God's new world.

I've sat with thirteen-year-olds who told me what it was like to see their dad hit their mom.
I've listened to eighteen-year-old girls talk about what it was like to be raped.
I've heard a mother describe what's it's like to hear her five-year-old boy, whose father has just committed suicide, ask, "When is daddy coming home?"
I've sat with kids addicted to cocaine who have that ravaged, empty look in their eyes that haunts you for days.

I've seen what happens when people abandon all that
is good and right and kind and humane.

I tell these stories because it is absolutely vital that
we acknowledge that love and grace and kindness
and compassion and humanity and everything
that Jesus invites us to can be rejected. From the
most subtle rolling of the eyes to the most violent
degradation of another human being, we are free to
reject God's will. As the first Christians wrote in the
New Testament, God turns us loose to do whatever
we want. We are free to pursue whatever evil we
desire.

Earlier we explored a bit about heaven.
Now let's explore a bit about hell,
because hell is what happens when we reject God's
invitation to be a part of God's new world.

We're free to make choices,
to live how we want,
to treat others, ourselves, and the earth
however we'd like.
And when we reject God's way,
we don't bring heaven to earth,
we bring hell to earth.

So is there a literal hell?
Let me answer that question with a question:
Those kids I saw in Rwanda, the ones missing arms
and legs because they'd been hacked off with a
machete, were those literal arms and legs?

Yes, they were.
And yes, there's a literal hell.
We see it every day—
every tear shed over a divorce, every bomb dropped
on an innocent family, every kid we see who's gotten
sucked into doing or dealing drugs . . . we see literal
hells every single day.

We experience hell on earth all the time.
Sometimes it's choices we make,
other times it's things people do to us,
sometimes it's the circumstances that seem to
conspire against us.
(We even have phrases for this agony: We say we're
having a hell of a time or we're going through hell.)
When someone pursues a destructive course of
action and they can't be convinced to change course,
we often say they're hell-bent on it—fixed, obsessed,
unshakable in their pursuit, unwavering in their

commitment to a destructive action.

Ever had a friend like that? One who kept making destructive choices no matter what you said or how passionately you tried to convince them to ease up?

It's so excruciating to watch, isn't it? That's because you're seeing hell on earth.

So when people say they don't believe in hell and they don't like the word "sin," my first response often is to ask, "Have you sat with a teen brother and sister who just found out that their dad has been cheating on their mom for years, and he's now leaving them to start another family with his new girlfriend?"

Sin is real,
and so is hell.
Right here, right now,
all around us.

Some words are strong for a reason. We need those words to be that intense, that loaded, that complex because they need to reflect the realities they describe.

If someone set your house on fire after stealing your

most valuable possessions, would you say that they have been inconsiderate?

No! You'd use a stronger word! Probably one with four letters!

Some agony needs agonizing language.
Some destruction does make you think of fire.
Some betrayal actually feels like we've been burned.
Some injustices do cause things to heat up.

For many people in our world, the only way they've ever heard hell talked about is the place reserved for those who don't believe, who haven't joined the church, who aren't Christians. Often the word "hell" is used by Christians talking about people who aren't Christians going to hell when they die, because they don't believe the right things.

But if you read all the passages in which Jesus uses the word "hell," we see something different. In the vast majority of these passages, he's talking to very devoted, religious Jewish people. He's talking to people who saw themselves as God's people. His audience was people who would say they were devoted believers. They were secure in their knowledge that they were God's chosen people. Jesus doesn't talk to them about "beliefs" as we think of them—he talks about anger and lust and violence and indifference. He talks about their hearts, about how they conduct themselves, how they interact with their neighbors, about the kind of effect they have on the world. What is so striking is that people believing the right or wrong things isn't his point.

Jesus did not use hell to try to scare "unbelievers" into believing. He talked about hell to very religious people to warn them about the consequences of straying from their God-given calling to show the world God's love.

This not to say that hell is not a giant warning or that it isn't intimately connected with what we believe, but simply to point out that when Jesus talked about hell, he was talking to very religious people who believed they were "in" with God. He warned them that their hard hearts and their failure to be loving witnesses to God's new work in the world were taking them down a very, very destructive and dangerous path.

I point this out because this takes us back to the

original invitation of Jesus—to trust him and believe him and commit ourselves to learning from him how to be his kind of people in the world.

This invitation can be accepted,
and it can be rejected,
because God respects our ability to choose.

We are that free.
Heaven,
or hell.
We can say yes to the invitation to come to the party,
or we can reject the invitation.
Our choice.

CHAPTER 4
QUESTIONS, QUESTIONS, QUESTIONS . . .

So, up to this point in the book we've explored heaven and hell and Jesus and his invitation to the party and the power of our choices—all of which can raise lots and lots of questions. I could, of course, keep writing like I've been doing, with paragraphs and ideas and insights and stories, but I'm betting, based on where we've been so far, that you're probably like my friend Kate, who would have lots of questions by now. She's a high school student who's funny and smart and loves to have discussions about faith and the big questions of life. She'd most likely have stopped me already and said, "But what about . . ."

So here's what we'll do: We'll tackle some of the questions Kate would have, because I bet you have some of the exact same ones, and I'll do my best to respond to each one as best I can and we'll see where it takes us.

Sound good?
Here's the first one:

So what happens when we die?
Great question. I don't know.

No, seriously, what happens?
I'm totally serious. I don't know. And the reason I don't know is because nobody knows. No one—at least that I've heard of, although there's probably something on YouTube! (that was a joke)—has ever died and brought back a picture of what happens when we die.

But lots of Christians are really, really confident that they know what is going to happen when they die—
Yes, they are. The problem is, they don't know. When we talk about what happens when we die, we're speculating. We don't have firm or provable evidence;

we have hunches and beliefs and theories and faith. No matter how much we quote Bible verses or creeds or doctrines or trusted authority figures, the honest truth is that when we talk about what happens when we die, we are all—from pastors to scholars to theologians to your friends to people on the internet to your family member giving a eulogy at a funeral— just speculating.

What we have is faith. And that's huge. That's massive. That's the difference, in my opinion. Because I believe in Jesus and I believe that God is the kind of God Jesus says God is, I have faith that when I die, I'll be with God. And faith is a beautiful thing; it can change your life.

But isn't the Christian faith about believing in Jesus so that when you die, you're with God?
The Christian faith is about Jesus—the person, the savior, the one who we can trust to do for us what we could never do for ourselves. The Christian faith is about trusting Jesus right now with your life, following him and allowing him to shape you into the kind of person God created you to be. That, of course, includes death, but it's much more about life. Life now, and life after death as well.

So everybody's speculating?

When it comes to what happens when we die, yes. But that doesn't mean that our beliefs and faith about what happens when we die don't matter. When you believe that God can be trusted and a new world is bursting forth right here in the midst of this one, it gives you a vision for life, a way of understanding who you are and what it means to be human. When you believe that Jesus has done for you what you could never do for yourself, when you come to see that God loves you exactly as you are, it profoundly affects how you live your life.

On the other hand, if you believe that when you die you go somewhere else and never again are a part of life on earth, then you won't be all that interested in partnering with God to help make the world the kind of place God intends for it to be.

But what about the comfort that believing we're going to heaven has brought to so many people— like those songs written by slaves in the Deep South about God relieving their suffering someday? Is belief in heaven okay?

Absolutely. It's incredibly important. It gives you

hope, which is one of the most valuable things a
person can have. It gives you motivation to work
for a better world. It gives you a vision of a better
tomorrow. It inspires you to make your life count. I
could go on. . . .

**Is this why in the first part of the book you talked
about heaven and hell as choices we make now?**
Yes, I've been trying to present heaven and hell, and
how I believe Jesus presented heaven and hell, as
two realities we choose between every single day.
Jesus was very insistent that now is the time to trust
him and enter into eternal life.

When Jesus spoke of hell, he used the word
"Gehenna." *Ge* means valley, and *henna* refers to
Hinnom. Gehenna was the Valley of Hinnom, an
actual valley that ran along the south and west sides
of the city of Jerusalem, the city Jesus visited often.
Gehenna was the town dump, where people threw
their trash, where there was a continual fire to burn
up the garbage. Of all the words Jesus could have
used to speak of hell, he used an actual place. It was
right over the wall of the city. People could see it.
People could literally see hell. The choices we make
and the actions we take have consequences, and

Jesus was very clear that some choices lead to really, really destructive consequences. Some choices lead to Gehenna.

So Jesus's message was mostly about this life?
Yes, I'd say that. He came from the Jewish tradition, which was much more concerned with being true to God right now, loving your neighbor, caring for the poor, and telling the truth. It was a tradition more concerned with the here and now than with speculating about what happens when you die. Have you ever noticed that the people who talk the most about going to heaven when you die seem to talk the least about bringing heaven to earth right now? And in the same way, have you noticed how the people who talk the most about going to hell when you die seem to talk much less about the very real hells on earth right now? I don't think that's what Jesus had in mind. I believe he wants us to take heaven and hell much more seriously here and now, trusting that he'll take care of us just fine when we die.

But what about what happens when we die—who will be with God?
Now that's a big question! I'll start by quoting a verse in the New Testament that says that "God wants all

people to be saved and to come to a knowledge of the truth." That's a really important place to begin answering the question, because the Bible is clear that God wants to have a relationship with everybody.

Got that? Everybody. No exceptions. That's what God wants. In fact, there's a verse in the letter to the Colossians that says that through Jesus' death on the cross, God is reconciling all things to God. All things—try and imagine that! God's desire is to have peace with every square inch of the universe. And then it's written in another verse that "God wanted to make the unchanging nature of God's purpose very clear." God has a purpose—saving and making peace with everybody—and that purpose has never changed, it involves everybody, and God's intention all along has been to communicate this intention clearly. The writers of the Bible consistently affirm that we're all part of the same family. What we have in common—regardless of our languages, customs, countries, beliefs, or religions—outweighs our differences. This is why God wants "all people to be saved."

Jesus tells a series of parables in Luke 15 about a woman who loses a coin, a shepherd who loses a sheep, and a father who loses a son. The stories aren't ultimately about things and people being lost; the stories are about things and people being found. The God Jesus teaches us about doesn't give up until everything that was lost is found. This God simply doesn't give up. Ever.

So everybody will be with God?

Certain traditions within the Christian faith believe that is what will happen eventually. They point to places in the Bible like Psalm 65, where it's written that "all people will come" to God and Ezekiel 36, where it's written that "the nations will know that I am the Lord." The prophet Isaiah said that "all people will see God's salvation."

And Paul wrote to the Philippians [2] that "Every knee shall bow and every tongue acknowledge." And then there's Psalm 22: "All the ends of the earth will remember and turn to the Lord, and all the families of the nations will bow down before him."

And then there are a number of passages where we find the phrase "all things"—Jesus spoke of the renewal of all things, Peter spoke of the restoration of all things, Paul wrote of the reconciliation of all things. These passages and others have led many to believe that given enough time, everybody will eventually turn to God and be in heaven-on-earth.

But what about Hitler and serial killers and devil-worshipping pedophiles? Even them?
That's the question lots of people have—myself included—and there are several ways to respond to it.

First, you can see why people believe in hell. People who are serious followers of Jesus believe God loves everybody and wants to be with everybody, but they believe in hell because they insist there must be a place for people who don't want to be with God. We've all observed people who seem to choose not to have anything to do with the things God calls us to— people who create lots of hells on earth—and so, the argument goes, because they don't want to be with God, God gives them what they want. That makes sense, doesn't it? That's seems totally possible.

Second, there is something I call the momentum theory. I explain it this way: Have you ever told a lie and then later found yourself telling another lie to cover up the first one? And then later, you found yourself trying to keep the lies straight in your head?

One lie often leads to another, which can easily lead to another.

No, let's think about this in regard to your life. If you develop destructive habits and patterns that continue on, year after year, it can get harder and harder and harder to do the right thing when the moment calls. It just gets more and more difficult to imagine any other kind of life. You can create a rut that can seem impossible to get out of. When we speculate about what happens when we die, it's important for us to keep in mind that choices have consequences that lead us somewhere. It's possible to make choices over the years to become the kind of person who doesn't want any part in heaven.

Kind of like the kid who starts cheating in school and does it for so long that he forgets how to actually study for a test?
Yes! Excellent example. You keep acting a certain way, and pretty soon it's the only way you know how to act. . . .

Yes, but you can always stop cheating and learn how to study! What about someone who does something really, really evil and destructive, something that

has consequences, something they can't just stop doing and it will all be fine?

You've raised a profound point there, and it's one I first heard my friend Matt talk about several years ago. Matt pointed out that in the first chapter of the Bible, it's written that we're all created in the image of God. We reflect in our creativity and compassion and spirit and love what God is like. Each of us has the choice in all we do to nurture and cultivate this divine image or to ignore it, deny it, and stifle it.

Ever notice that the organization that cares for animals is called the Humane Society? It's not a group dedicated to caring for people, so why is *humane* in their name? Because when a person abuses animals, something terrible happens to that person's humanity. Abusing animals is a less-than-human thing to do. So if we can become less and less humane in our treatment of animals or ourselves and others, what would happen if this behavior went on unchecked for years and years? Would a person's humanity eventually ebb away completely? Could a person reach the point where they no longer bore the image of God? Could the divine image be extinguished in a person, given enough time and neglect? Some have presented the possibility that a person could eventually move into a new state, one in which they were in essence "formerly human" or "post-human" or even "ex-human." This is why you often hear serial killers described as "monsters." They are something other than what you and I are. They are something indescribably awful, something no longer human.

Or to put it another way, in terms of a party: If you can say yes to the invitation to the party, then obviously you can say no to the invitation to the party. Those are choices we can make, and those choices take us in very specific directions.

So rejecting the invitation to the party is hell?
Yep. Remember, God is love, and love involves freedom. If you don't have the choice to love, then it isn't love. When you love someone or ask them out or move toward them, you have to give them the freedom to say no, to reject your love. Love is risky; there's no way around it.

So are you saying that for God to truly be loving, God has to give people the choice to reject God?
Exactly.

**So some Christians believe that everybody will
eventually be saved, and others believe that some
people will be in hell?**
Well, actually, those are only two of many options—
over the years people have answered these questions
about who goes where, when, why, and how in a
number of ways. Or to be more specific: Orthodox,
serious followers of Jesus have answered these
questions in radically different ways across the
ages. Or to say it another way: However you answer
these questions, you can probably find a group of
Christians who would answer in a similar way.

This diversity of perspectives isn't threatening.
It's liberating. If you have heard one of these
perspectives and it didn't work, it didn't bring life,
it didn't take you further into the heart of God, then
leave it behind. Drop it. Let it go.

This isn't because you aren't serious or you don't
believe or you've lost faith or you're on some sort of
slippery slope; it's because some beliefs bring life
and some don't. Some take us into the wonder and
beauty and power and peace and joy of God's love.
Others don't.

I have met a staggering number of people over the years who find Jesus compelling but don't follow him because of the parts about "God sending people to hell and tormenting them forever." Somewhere along the way, they were taught that the only option when it comes to the Christian faith is to clearly declare that a few, committed Christians will "go to heaven" when they die and everyone else will not. The matter is settled at death and that's it. One place or the other, no looking back, no chance for a change of heart. Make your bed now and lie in it . . . forever.

Not all Christians believe this—and more importantly, you don't have to believe it to be a Christian. The Christian faith is big enough, wide enough, and generous enough to handle that vast of a range of perspectives.

But the view that God will torture some people forever, how can anyone say that's a legitimate way to see God?
Great question, and one we'll deal with in detail later. But I'll say this here: It's important that we are honest about the fact that some stories are better that others. Telling a story in which billions of people spend forever somewhere in the universe trapped

in a black hole of endless torment and misery with
no way out isn't a very good story. Telling a story
about a God who inflicts unrelenting punishment on
people because they didn't do or say or believe the
correct things in a brief window of time called life is
a terrible story. On the flip side, everybody enjoying
God's good world together with justice being served
and all the wrongs being made right is a much
better, bigger, more loving story. It is more inspiring
than any other story. Whatever objections a person
might have to this story, one has to admit that it is
fitting, proper, and Christian to long for it. We can be
honest about the warped nature of the human heart,
the freedom that love requires, and the destructive
choices people make—and still trust that God's love
is bigger, stronger, and more compelling than all of
that put together. The grace of God demands we
leave lots of room here for a future that good.

It probably seems to some people that God couldn't
be that big or good or loving. . . .

Some faith is small and shrunken and pathetic. It's
lost the ability to imagine. There's a prayer in the
New Testament that's offered to the God who can do
"immeasurably more than we can ask or imagine."

What a great word, that word "imagine" there. And then more than that! More than our minds can handle. It makes sense, then, that the Christian story would begin with the straightforward affirmation that God is good, and whatever story God is telling in human history will be better than anything we ever thought possible.

But what about the verse where Jesus says he's the only way to God? Isn't that why those Christians hold up those signs in front of concerts about how everybody who doesn't believe in Jesus is going to hell?

It's important in answering the question to point out that when Jesus said no one comes to the father but through him, he wasn't saying that only Christians get to be with God. If that was the case, he could have said that exact thing! What he did say is that whatever God is doing to save the world is happening through him. Now that's something very different. What I find incredibly fascinating in the stories about Jesus is that when he does talk about the future, he tells a lot of stories that are about surprise. In one instance he told a story about people invited into "the kingdom prepared for you since the creation of the world" and their first reaction is . . . surprise. They start asking questions, trying to figure it out. It's not a story of people boldly walking in through the pearly gates, confident that they'll be welcomed in because of their faith. It's a story about people saying:

"What? Us? When did we ever see you? What did we ever do to deserve it?"

Heaven, it turns out, is full of the unexpected. Jesus told another story about a great banquet a man gave, and how the people who would normally attend such a feast had better things to do. So, in their absence, the host invites all the people from the streets and alleyways who would never attend a party like this.

Unexpected, surprising—not what you'd think. These aren't isolated impulses in Jesus' outlook, they're the themes he comes back to again and again. He tells entire villages full of extremely devoted religious people that they're in danger, while seriously questionable "sinners" will be better off than them in that day.

What about people who don't say they're Christians but act more like Jesus than people who do say they're Christians?
I've seen that a lot. What we have to keep in mind

is that some people have really, really terrible associations with the word "Jesus." Some were abused by a "Christian" relative, others were taught that to be a Christian meant you were a racist or you had to deny basic science—for some the word "Jesus" is jumbled up with lots of other things that have nothing to do with Jesus. Lots of wise, insightful Christians over the years have pointed out that people respond to the light wherever they find it. Some are responding to Jesus. They just don't call it that. At least for now.

So you're saying we should be skeptical of whatever religious system people create to decide who's in and who's out?
Let me tell you a story to answer that: Several years ago at the church I was a part of, we had an art show. One artist included in her piece a quote from Mahatma Gandhi, which a number of people found quite compelling. But not everyone. Someone attached a piece of paper to it. On the piece of paper was written: *Reality check: He's in hell.*

Really?
Gandhi's in hell?
He is?

We have confirmation of this?
Somebody knows this?
For sure?
And they decided to let the rest of us know?

We don't know who is where in the afterlife—and
it can be really damaging to make those kinds of
judgments, and it can turn lots of people off to
Jesus and his message.

Making judgment about things we don't know
anything about simply isn't our job.

**Does that mean that some people who have never
heard about Jesus can get a second chance to
believe in him after they die?**
Some believe that God will wait for as long as it
takes, even if that takes many years. Others present
the idea that some people may have been responding
to Jesus, saying yes to him, but they didn't know it
was him.

Others say that we can confidently trust that because
God wants to save everybody, God will never stop
doing everything God can do to have a relationship
with us.

So Gandhi will eventually become a Christian?
You know what? God loves Gandhi just like God loves you and me and every single other person who's ever lived, and that's enough for me. It's not our job to try to figure all that out. Gandhi is in good hands.

But if people get a second chance after they die, then why does it matter how you live now?
This is an incredibly important question that lots of people ask. It reveals a massive misunderstanding of who God is and what it means to follow Jesus!

I respond to it like this: If I told you that there was a million dollars buried in your backyard, what would you do?

Exactly! You'd stop reading and start digging, right? My announcement of what is already yours would create within you not laziness or complacency but incredible, intense urgency.

The good news that Jesus brings us has that kind of effect—you want to tell everybody, and you want to find your role in the story God is telling.

But what about the people who say that you need

to warn people about hell, otherwise they won't be motivated to believe?
You're right, people do say that, usually in response to the idea that people get a second or third or millionth chance to believe in Jesus after they die. The idea behind that idea is that if people aren't scared of going to hell, then they'll have no motivation to live how God wants them to live. That implies that if you don't *have* to do the right thing now, you won't do the right thing now.

That reveals a horrible view of God: namely, that the only way God can get people to change their ways is to threaten them with torture.

This is the exact opposite of Jesus's message: He comes to give us a vision of life so beautiful and compelling and fascinating and fulfilling that our hearts want nothing more.

Some schools require that their students do community service projects as part of their grades. It can be a really great experience to volunteer in a homeless shelter or to visit the elderly or to clean up a park. But that's a very different thing from doing it simply because you want to.

Do you see how some of the questions people ask reveal what they really think Jesus came to do? He didn't come to threaten us with punishment or to mark us down if we don't participate. He came to change our hearts.

But if he didn't come to warn us about hell, then why are Christians so fixated on sharing their faith, like the kids who keep inviting other students to their youth group?
Actually, I think he does come to warn us about hell—the thousands of hells that are around us right now. Think about attending your favorite concert— what did you do countless times throughout the show? You took photos and posted them to Facebook, or maybe you texted them to friends. You wanted people to see and experience what you were experiencing, because you were enjoying it so much. When your heart has been captured, your natural response is to share that with people.

You keep talking about this kind of life Jesus invites us into—how do we get it? Do we have to say a prayer or do a ritual or read something or believe something?
There are lots of answers to that question, but I'll

give you just one way to think about it. Jesus often began his speeches by telling people that they need to have a whole new mind, to turn around in their thinking and head in the other direction. And to see things in a whole new way means you have to stop seeing them the old way. To turn in a new direction means you have to stop going in the other direction. That's why I've framed this whole book in terms of an invitation to a party. To say yes to the party means you leave what you're doing and come to the party!

It's that simple?
Yes, and no.

Yes, because Jesus insists that God's grace and forgiveness are for all of us and cover over every single solitary thing we've ever done wrong. I remember going through a process with a group of teens who were struggling with destructive choices they'd made. We literally had a ceremony where they wrote down their greatest regrets, and then we set the pile of papers on fire. It was so moving to see them let go of their pasts.

But the answer is also no, because sometimes

we've done things that have affected other people in negative ways. So part of getting right with God is getting right with other people we've wronged, going to them and asking for their forgiveness and doing what we can to make amends.

But what about the reality of hell when you die? Does this mean we can take hell less seriously?
No, because, no offense, there's an even better question: What about hell now? Jesus wants to rescue people now.

It's amazing how many questions all this raises.
Yep. And we're just getting started! Here's a few more:

Of all the billions of people who have ever lived, will only a select number make it to a better place and every single other person suffer in torment and punishment forever? Is this acceptable to God?
Why them?
Why you?
Why me?

Does God punish people for thousands of years with infinite, eternal punishment for things they did in their few finite years of life?

If only a select few go to heaven and billions burn forever, the odds are most people won't make it!

So how does a person end up being one of the few?
Chance?
Luck?
Random selection?
Being born in the right place, family, or country?
Having a youth pastor who "relates better to the kids"?
God choosing you instead of others?

What kind of faith is that?
Or more importantly,
what kind of God is that?

And whenever people claim that one group is in, saved, accepted by God, forgiven, enlightened, redeemed—and everybody else isn't—why is it that those who make this claim are almost always part of the group that's "in"?

Have you ever heard people make claims about a select few being chosen and then claim that they're not part of that group?

Several years ago I heard a woman tell about the funeral of her daughter's friend, a high school student who was killed in a car accident. Her daughter was asked by a Christian if the young man who had died was a Christian. She said that he told people he was an atheist. This person then said to her, "So there's no hope then."

No hope?
Is that the Christian message?
Is that what Jesus offers the world, no hope?

And what exactly does happen when a fifteen-year-old atheist dies? What if he would have become religious the week after he died? Is it really his fault that he hadn't had the time to say the right prayer or take the right class or join the right church or have something happen somewhere in his heart? He gets an eternity in hell because he couldn't find God before he turned fifteen?

So what do we do with all these questions?

My response is to take us back to Jesus's message, which always leads us to the openness of our hearts and our love for our neighbor and our trust that God is doing something in the world. And the best part is that we can be a part of it.

But isn't that a cop-out for having real answers, which is what religion is supposed to do?
No, that's a distorted view of religion. It's really, really important that we're clear about this: Jesus didn't come promising all the answers; he came promising full, abundant, vibrant life. He came to offer water to the thirsty.

My friend John Shore is very good at coming up with metaphors to explain why things are the way they are, and he says it's like a museum with beautiful paintings on the walls, but in one corner there's a door that's locked. You're wandering around the museum, and you come across this door that you can't open. And so you try harder and harder and harder. You're yanking on it, trying to pick the lock, rattling the knob, kicking the jamb, and you still can't get it to open . . . because it's locked. The door is locked because whoever runs the museum doesn't want you going in there. The point of the museum is to enjoy the art on the walls, not the art you can't see.

Fact is: Some doors are just locked. We can speculate about why, but when it comes to the afterlife and heaven and hell and who gets in and who doesn't, some doors are just locked. I believe God locked those doors so that we'd learn to be content with mystery, trusting Jesus, experiencing the life God has for us now, enjoying the art hanging on the walls.

Wow. This has been a lot of questions, and yet it feels like we're just getting started. . . .
I know! That's what faith is supposed to be like! Invigorating, live-giving, interesting, provocative, unexpected, challenging. You never come to the end of all there is to discover and learn and explore and experience . . . but hopefully we've gotten a good start here.

Now, let's move to the next chapter and talk about stories.

CHAPTER 5
THE STORY IN THE STORY

Now, let's talk about stories. Your story, my story, God's story, and a story Jesus told about a man who has two sons. In this story, the younger son demands his share of the father's inheritance early, and the father unexpectedly gives it to him. The son takes the money, leaves home, blows it all on meaningless living, and then returns home hoping to be hired as a worker in his dad's business. His father—again unexpectedly—welcomes his son home and throws him a homecoming party.

A party that his older brother refuses to join.

It's unfair, the older brother tells his father. He's never been given so much as a goat, not to mention a huge homecoming party. The father then says to him, "You are always with me, and everything I have is yours. But we had to celebrate and be glad, because this brother of yours was dead and is alive again; he was lost and is found."

I retell this story of Jesus', because of the number of stories being told in this one story.

The younger brother tells his version of the story. He heads home in shame after squandering his father's money, rehearsing the speech he'll give his father. He is convinced he's "no longer worthy" to be called his father's son. That's the story he's telling, that's the one he's believing. It's stunning, then, when he gets home and his father demands that the best robe be put on him and a ring placed on his finger and sandals on his feet. Robes and rings and sandals are signs of being a son. Although he's decided he can't be a son anymore, his father tells a different story about him. One about return and reconciliation and redemption. One about his being a son again.

The younger son has to decide whose version of his

story he's going to trust: his or his father's. One in which he is no longer worthy to be called a son or one in which he's a robe-, ring-, and sandal-wearing son who was dead but is alive again, who was lost but has now been found.

There are two versions of his story.
His.
And his father's.

He has to choose which one he will live in.
Which one he will believe.
Which one he will trust.

The same, it turns out, is true for his older brother. He, too, has a version of the story. He tells his father, "All these years I've been slaving for you and never disobeyed your orders. Yet you never gave me even a young goat so I could celebrate with my friends. But when this son of yours . . ."

(He can't even say his brother's name. That's when you know you're in deep, when hate and bitterness and spite have got you by the throat, when you can't even say your own brother's name.)

". . . who has squandered your property with prostitutes comes home, you kill the fattened calf for him!"

There's so much there in those few words, isn't there?
You get the sense that he's been saving it up for years, and now out it comes.

In his version of events, he's been slaving for his father for years. That's how he describes life in his father's house: slaving. That directly contradicts the few details we've been given about the father, who appears to be anything but a slave driver.

Second, he says his father has never even given him a goat. A goat doesn't have much meat on it, so even in conjuring up an image of celebration, it's meager. Lean. Lame. The kind of party he envisions just isn't that impressive. What he reveals here is what he really thinks about his father: He thinks he's cheap.

Third, he claims that his father has dealt with his brother according to a totally different set of standards. He thinks his father is unfair. He thinks he's been wronged, shorted, shafted. And he's furious about it.

All with the party in full swing in the background.

The father isn't rattled or provoked. He simply responds, "My son, you are always with me, and everything I have is yours." And then he tells him that they have to celebrate.

You are always with me, and everything I have is yours.

In one sentence, the father manages to tell an entirely different story about the older brother.

First, the father insists that the son hasn't been a slave, he's had it all the whole time. There's been no need to work, obey orders, or slave away to earn what he's had the whole time.

Second, the father hasn't been cheap with him. He could have had whatever he wanted whenever he wanted it. Everything the father owns has always been his. All he had to do was receive.

Third, the father redefines fairness. It's not that the father has been unfair with him; it's that his father never set out to be fair in the first place. Grace and generosity aren't fair; that's their very essence. The father sees the younger brother's return as one more occasion to practice *unfairness*. The younger son doesn't deserve a party—that's the point of the party. That how things work in the father's world. Profound unfairness.

People get what they don't deserve.
Parties are thrown for younger brothers who squander their inheritance.

After all,
"you are always with me, and everything I have is yours."

What the father does is retell the older brother's story, just as he did with the younger brother. The question, then, is the same question that confronted the younger brother—will he trust his version of his story or his father's version of his story?

Who will he trust?
What will he believe?

The difference between the two stories is,

after all,
the difference between heaven and hell.

Here's what I mean by that:
Most people think of heaven and hell in terms of
separation, with one
"up" there
and the other
"down" there.

(Wherever here and there are!)

Two different places,
far apart from each other.

Jesus, however, does something very different here in
this story. Jesus puts the older brother right there at
the party, welcomed and invited, but refusing to trust
the father's version of the story. Which means he's
refusing to join in the celebration.

Hell is being at the party but refusing to join it.
That's what makes it so hellish.

It's not an image of separation, but one of
integration—the two realities of heaven and hell are

right there in each other's presence. In this story, heaven and hell are within each other, intertwined, interwoven, bumping up against each other.

Hell is our refusal to trust God's retelling of our story. We all have our version of events. Who we are, who we aren't, what we've done, what that means for our future. Beliefs about our worth, value, and significance. The things we think are true about ourselves that we cling to despite the pain and agony they cause.

If you've ever had a friend who was thinking of suicide, then you know exactly what I'm talking about. You go over to her house and you know she's in trouble, and she tells you how down she is and that she doesn't know if it's worth it and how no one loves her and that she's a failure. What do you do? You grab her by the shoulders and look her in the eyes, and you tell her that she matters and that she's loved and that she's not a failure. She has to keep going, no matter how hard it is.

You realize what's going on in that moment, don't you? You're doing what God does; you're retelling the story. She's suicidal because she's been believing a particular story about herself, a depressing, despairing, soul-killing story that reminds us how important our beliefs truly are. What you're doing in that moment is confronting her with another story about who you believe she is, and you're begging her to believe it!

Some people are haunted by sins of the past. Flaws, failures, shame—like a stain that won't wash out. Some have a deep-seated, profound belief that they are, at some primal level of the soul, not good enough.

For others, it isn't their acute sense of their lack or inadequacy or sins; it's their pride. Their ego. They're convinced of their own greatness and autonomy. They don't need anybody. Often the belief is that God, Jesus, church, etc., are for the "weak ones" who can't make it in the world. They cling to religious superstitions and myths like a drug, a crutch, a way to avoid taking responsibility for their pathetic lives.

We believe all sorts of things about ourselves.

What the gospel does is confront us with God's version of our own story.

It is a brutally honest,
exuberantly liberating story,
and it is good news.

It begins with the sure and certain truth that we are
loved.

In spite of whatever has gone horribly wrong deep
in our hearts and has spread to every corner of the
world,
in spite of our sins,
failures,
rebellion,
and hard hearts,
in spite of what's been done to us
or what we've done,
God has made peace with us.

Done. Complete.
As Jesus said, "It is finished."

We are now invited to live a whole new life without
guilt or shame or blame or anxiety. We are going to
be fine. Of all the images of God, of all the language
Jesus could put on the lips of the God character in
this story he tells, he has the father say,

"You are always with me, and everything I have is yours."

The older brother has been clinging to his version of events for so long, it's hard for him to conceive of any other way of seeing things.

And so the father's words, which are generous and loving, are also difficult and shocking.

Again, we create hell whenever we fail to trust God.

The older brother's failure to trust, we learn, is rooted in a distorted view of his father. There's a problem with his understanding of who his father even is.

This perspective of the older brother has everything to do with our story. Millions of people in our world have been told that God so loved the world that God sent Jesus to save us, rescue us, and give us this love. When we accept and believe in Jesus, then we'll have a relationship with God.

Good news, so far.

But there's more. Millions of people have been taught that if you don't believe, if you don't accept in the right way—that is, the way the person telling them understands the gospel—and you were hit by a car and died later that same day, God would have no choice but to punish you forever in hell. God would, in essence, become a fundamentally different being to you in that moment of death and a different being to you forever after. A loving heavenly father who will go to extraordinary lengths to have a relationship with you would, in the blink of an eye, become a cruel, mean, vicious tormenter who would ensure that there is no escape from an endless future of agony.

If there was an earthly father who was like that, we would call the authorities. If there was an actual human dad who was that volatile, we would contact child protection services immediately.

If God can switch gears like that, switch entire modes of being that quickly, that raises a thousand questions about whether a being like this could ever be trusted, let alone be good.

Loving one moment, vicious the next.

Kind and compassionate, only to become cruel and relentless moments later.

Does God become somebody totally different the moment you die?

That kind of God is devastating.
Psychologically crushing.
We can't bear it.
No one can.

And that's the secret deep in the heart of many people, especially Christians: They don't love God. They can't, because the God they've been presented with and taught about can't be loved. That God is terrifying and traumatizing and unbearable.

And there are conferences about how churches can be more relevant and reach more young people and be more welcoming. There are vast resources—books and films and such—for those who want to build relationships with people who aren't part of the church. And that can be really helpful. But at the heart of it, we have to ask: Just what kind of God is behind all this?

Because if something is wrong with your God,
if your God is loving one second and cruel the next,
if your God will punish people for all of eternity for
sins committed in a few short years,
no amount of clever marketing
or compelling language
or good music
or great coffee
will be able to disguise
that one, true, glaring, untenable, unacceptable,
awful reality.

Hell is refusal to trust, and refusing to trust is often
rooted in a distorted view of God. Sometimes the
reason people have a problem accepting "the gospel"
is that they sense that the God lurking behind Jesus
isn't safe, loving, or good. It doesn't make sense, it
can't be reconciled, and so they say no. They don't
want anything to do with Jesus, because they don't
want anything to do with that God.

What we see with the older brother is that our beliefs
matter. What we believe about who we are and how
we've been treated and whether we think God has
been good to us or not, our beliefs deeply shape how
we live.

We can trust God's retelling of our story,
or we can cling to our version of our story.
And to trust God's retelling,
we have to trust God.

Several truths are important here:
First, one about our choices.
We are free to accept or reject the invitation to the
new life that God extends to us.
Our choice.

We're at the party,
but we don't have to join in.
Heaven or hell.
Both at the party.

To reject God's grace,
to turn from God's love,
to resist God's telling,
will lead to misery.
It is a form of punishment, all on its own.

This is an important distinction, because in talking
about what God is like, we cannot avoid the realities
of God's very essence, which is love. It can be
resisted and rejected and denied, and that resisting,

denying, and rejection will bring another reality.
We are that free.

When people say they're tired of hearing about "sin"
and "judgment" and "condemnation," it's often
because those have been confused for them with the
nature of God. God has no desire to inflict pain or
agony on anyone. God extends an invitation to us,
and we are free to do with it as we please.

Saying yes will take us in one direction;
saying no will take us in another.

God is love,
and to refuse this love moves us away from it,
in the other direction,
and that will,
by its very definition,
bring you to an increasingly unloving hellish reality.

We do ourselves great harm when we confuse the
very nature of God, which is love, with the very real
consequences of rejecting and resisting that love,
which creates what we call hell.

Second, another distinction to be clear about, one

between entrance and enjoyment.
God is love,
and "love" requires a relationship.
And this relationship is one of joy.
It can't be contained.

Like when you see something amazing—my friends
and I were surfing yesterday, and the waves were big
and the water was warm and clear and there were
dolphins swimming by, and we kept saying to each
other, "How great is this?"

Think about that question for a minute, because I
know you've had similar experiences before, where
you and your friends are encountering something so
great that you turn to each other and ask, "Isn't this
amazing?" Why do we ask that question?

Because that question is actually an invitation. We're
asking, but we're really inviting our friends to join
us in our joy and wonder and pleasure. Our own
experience of the event can't be contained within it;
we just have to share it.

That's the feeling in the first chapters of the Bible.
Creating brings God such joy that God can't help but

want others to share in that joy. Sometimes people get into deep discussions about why humans exist and why were we created, and I think one of the best answers is: because God is pure joy and wants to share it with others. That's how joy and pleasure and amazement work.

Jesus invites us into that relationship, the one at the center of the universe. He insists that he's one with God, that we can be one with him, and that life is a generous, abundant reality. This God Jesus spoke of has always been looking for partners, people passionate about participating in the ongoing creation of the world.

So when the gospel is diminished down to a question of whether or not a person will get into heaven, that reduces the good news to a ticket, a way to get past the bouncer and into the club.

The good news is better than that.

This is why Christians who talk the most about going to heaven while everybody else goes to hell don't throw very good parties.

When the gospel is understood primarily in terms of entrance rather than joyous participation, it can actually serve to cut us off from the explosive, liberating experience of the God who is an endless, giving circle of joy and creativity.

Life has never been about just getting in. It's about thriving in God's good world. It's stillness, peace, and that feeling of your soul being at rest. At the same time it's about asking things, learning things, creating things, and sharing our creations with others who are finding the same kind of joy in the same good world.

Jesus calls disciples to keep entering into this shared life of peace and joy as it transforms our hearts, until it's the most natural way to live that we can imagine, until it's second nature, until we naturally embody the kind of attitudes that will go on in the age to come.

When people have been taught that the point of life is to get out of here and just *get into* heaven, they rarely create good art or innovate or contribute to the world like they could. It's a cheap view of the world, because it's a cheap view of God.

When you've experienced the resurrected Jesus, the mystery hidden in the fabric of creation, you can't help but talk about him. You've tapped into the joy that fills the entire universe, and so naturally you want others to meet this God. This is a God worth telling people about.

This is what I've learned as a pastor talking with people about God over the years: Lots of people were taught about a God who is mean and nasty and quite terrifying. Lots of people have been taught that whatever they're doing and however hard they're trying, God's attitude toward them is basically, "You're not doing enough."

As in, not going to church enough, not reading the Bible enough, not good enough, strong enough, nice enough, selfless enough. The God they've been taught about is like a slave driver who is never pleased or satisfied with you.

So why would anyone want to tell others about that God?

But when you realize that God is love, and you have experienced this love in flesh and blood, here and now, then you are freed from guilt and fear and that terrifying, haunting, ominous voice that whispers over your shoulder, "You aren't doing enough."

We're invited to trust the retelling now,
so that we're already taking part in the world to come.

This leads to another important point: Many people have had the message of Jesus explained to them as a rescue. They were taught that God *has* to punish sinners, because God is holy, but Jesus has paid the price for our sin so we can have eternal life. What this way of explaining Jesus's message can subtly do is teach that what Jesus does is rescue us from God.

Let's be very clear: We do not need to be rescued from God. God is the one who rescues us.

We shape our God, and then our God shapes us. Inquisitions, persecutions, trials, book burnings, blacklisting—when religious people become violent, it is because they have been shaped by their God, who is violent. I recently met a teen who's had some really mean Christians posting really mean things on her Facebook page because of the church she goes to— they don't think it's true enough or spiritual enough or something. (Their arguments made no sense to her!)

It's as if the girl's religion has turned them into spiritual bullies. For some, the highest form of allegiance to their God is to attack, defame, and slander others who don't believe exactly as they do. They're threatened by any faith that doesn't look exactly like theirs—which of course makes their faith less and less appealing to those around them.

We shape our God, and then our God shapes us. A distorted understanding of God, clung to with white knuckles and fierce determination, can leave a person outside the party, mad about a party, with a goat they're convinced they missed out on.

Jesus was very clear that this destructive, violent understanding of God can easily be institutionalized—in churches, systems, and ideas. It's important that we're honest about this, because some churches are not life-giving places. They drain people of life until there's very little left. That God is angry, demanding, a slave driver, and so that God's religion becomes a system of sin management. For that God, we are constantly angling to avoid what surely must be coming—the wrath that follows every sin.

There is another dimension to the violent, demanding God, the one people need Jesus to rescue them from. We see it in the words of the older brother, when he says he "never disobeyed." It's like the kid who's just been caught smoking in the bathroom, and now he's saying there's no sign that says he can't. You can sense the anxiety in his defense. There's a paranoid awareness that he believed his father was looking over his shoulder the whole time, just waiting to catch him. The violent God creates profound worry in people. Stress. This God promises peace, that's how the pitch goes, but in the end this God only produces followers who are paranoid or paralyzed. Whatever you do, don't step out of line. Don't give this God reason to be displeased, because who knows what will be unleashed.

Jesus frees us from that, because his love simply does away with fear.

Each brother has his own version of events,
his own telling of his story.
But their stories are distorted,
because they misunderstand the nature of their father—we've seen that.

But there's another reason their stories aren't true, a reason rooted less in the nature of God and more in the sons' beliefs about themselves.

The younger brother believes that he is cut off, estranged, and no longer deserves to be his father's son, because of all the terrible things he's done.

His badness is his problem, he thinks.

He's blown the money on meaningless living until he was facedown in the gutter, dragging his family name through the mud in the process. He is convinced that his destructive deeds have put him in such a bad state that he doesn't even deserve to be called a son anymore.

The older brother believes that the reason he deserves to be a son is because of all the good he's done, all the rules he's obeyed, all the days he's slaved for his father.

He thinks he deserves to be a son because of his goodness.

The younger brother's wrongs have led him away

from home, away from the family, deep into misery. His sins have separated him from his father.

The second truth, the one that is much more subtle and toxic, is that the older brother is separated from the father as well, even though he stayed home.

His problem is his goodness. His confidence in his rule keeping and law abiding has actually separated him from his father.

What we learn in his speech to his father is that he has been operating under the assumption that his years of service and slaving were actually earning him good standing with his father.

He thinks his father loves him because of how obedient he's been. He think he's deserving because of all the work he's done. He thinks his father owes him.

Our badness can separate us from God's love, that's clear.
But our goodness can separate us from God's love as well.

Do you see yourself in either of these sons?

Neither son understands that the father's love was never about any of that. Their father's love could never be earned, and it can never be taken away.

It just is.

It has no beginning and it has no end.

It goes on,
well into the night,
and into the next day,
and the next,
and the next,
without any finish in sight.

Your deepest, darkest sins and your shameful secrets are simply irrelevant when it comes to the counterintuitive, ecstatic announcement of the gospel.

So are your goodness, your rightness, your church attendance, your after-school activities, all the wise, moral decisions you have made and smart, mature actions you have taken.

It doesn't matter when it comes to the surprising, unexpected declaration that God's love is simply yours.

There is nothing left for both sons to do but trust that what the father keeps insisting is true about them is actually true. As it's written in the New Testament [Philippians 3:16], "let us live up to what we have already attained."

The father has taken care of everything.
It's all there,
ready,
waiting.
It's always been there,
ready,
waiting.

Our trusting,
our change of heart,
our believing God's version of our story doesn't bring it into existence, make it happen, or create it.

It simply is.

On the cross, Jesus said,

Father, forgive them, for they don't know what they're doing [Luke 23].

Jesus forgives them all,
without their asking for it.
Done.
Taken care of.
Before we could be good enough or right enough.
Before we could even believe the right things.

God isn't waiting for us to get it together,
to clean up, shape up, get up—
God has already done it.
Not because of anything good we've done,
while we were still powerless.
God is not counting our sins against us.

Jesus meets and redeems us in all the ways we have it together and in all the ways we don't, in all the times we proudly display for the world our goodness, greatness, and rightness, and in all the ways we fall flat on our faces.

It's only when you lose your life that you can find it, Jesus says.

The only thing left to do is trust.
Everybody is already at the party.
Heaven and hell,
here,
now,
around us,
upon us,
within us.

CHAPTER 6
TIME FOR THE PARTY

And so we arrive at the last chapter. The end is here.
We've explored a fairly vast expanse of topics, from
heaven and hell to God, Jesus, joy, violence, and
why the good news is better than we may have ever
imagined.

I've often talked through this book about a party,
a party that everybody, everywhere, is invited to, a
party that has already started and goes on and on
and on.

A story, then, about this party.

One night when I was in elementary school, I said a prayer kneeling beside my bed in my room in the farmhouse we lived in on Dobie Road in Okemos, Michigan. With my parents on either side of me, I invited Jesus into my heart. I told God that I believed that I was a sinner and that Jesus came to save me and I wanted to be a Christian.

I still remember that prayer.
It did something to me.
Something in me.
In an innocent, grade-school kind of way, I believed that God loved me and that Jesus came to show me that love and that I was being invited to accept that love.

Now, I am well aware of how shaped I was by my environment, how young and naïve I was, and how easy it is to discount emotional religious experiences. With very little effort a person can deconstruct an experience like that by pointing out all the other things going on in that prayer—the desire to please one's parents and the power of religion to shape a child. But however helpful that may be, it can easily miss the one thing that can't be denied: What happened that night was real. It meant something significant then, and it continues to have profound significance for me. That prayer was a defining moment in my life.

I tell you that story because I believe that the indestructible love of God is an unfolding, dynamic reality and that every single one of us is endlessly being invited to trust, accept, believe, embrace, and experience it. Whatever words you find helpful for describing this act of trust, Jesus invites us to say yes to this love of God, again and again and again.

Over the years I have had lots of doubts, I have asked lots of questions, I have done lots of exploring, I have tried lots of things, always searching for meaning and hope and significance. I have learned that there is a temptation at times to become hostile to our earlier understandings, feeling embarrassed that we were so "simple" or "naïve" or "brainwashed" or whatever terms arise when we haven't come to terms with our own story. These past understandings aren't to be denied or dismissed. They're to be embraced. Those experiences belong. Love demands that they belong. That's where we were at that point in our life. God met us there. Those moments were necessary for us to arrive here, at this place, at this time, as we are. Love frees us to embrace all of our history, the history in which all things are being made new.

Our invitation, the one that is offered to us with each and every breath, is to trust that we are loved and that a new word has been spoken about us, a new story is being told about us.

Now that word "trust," that is a rare, difficult word.

Cynicism we know, and skepticism we're familiar with. We know how to analyze and pick apart and point out inconsistencies. We're good at it. We've all been burned,
promised any number of things only to be let down. And so over time we get our guard up, we don't easily believe anything, and trust can become like a foreign tongue, a language we used to speak, but now we find ourselves out of practice.

This is especially true when you're in your teens and you're living under someone else's roof and you're trying to figure out what's true and what's real and what you're going to make your own.

Jesus invites us to trust that the love we fear is too good to be true is actually good enough to be true. It's written in one of John's letters in the scriptures that "what we will be has not yet been made known." Jesus invites us to become, to be drawn into this love as it shapes us and forms us and takes over every square inch of our lives. Jesus calls us to repent, to have our minds and hearts transformed, so that we see everything differently.

It will require a death,
a humbling,
a leaving behind of the old mind,
and at that same time it will require an opening up,
loosening our hold,
and letting go,
so that we can receive,
expand,
find,
hear,
see,
and enjoy.

This invitation to trust asks for nothing more than this moment, and yet it is infinitely urgent. Jesus told a number of stories in which people missed out on incredible opportunities because they didn't act when they had the chance.

We only get one life here and now.

Jesus tells these stories to wake us up to the timeless truth that history moves forward, not backward or sideways. Time does not repeat itself. Neither does life. While we continually find grace waiting to pick us up off the ground after we have fallen, there are realities to our choices. While we may get other opportunities, that specific moment will pass, and we will not see it again. It comes, it's here, it goes, and then it's gone. There are no second chances at the same moment. Jesus reminds us in a number of ways that it is vitally important that we take our choices here and now as seriously as we possibly can. They matter more than we can begin to imagine.

Whatever you've been told about your life,
I want you to know that God will give what you want.

God is that loving.

If you want isolation, despair, and the right to be

your own god, God will graciously grant you that
option. If you insist on using your God-given power
and strength to make the world in your own image,
God will allow you the freedom and the kind of space
where you can do that—alone, detached, and free
from any other people to get in your way. If you want
nothing to do with light, hope, love, grace, and peace,
God respects that desire on your part, and you'll be
given a life free from any of those realities. The more
you want nothing to do with who God is, the more
distance and space from God's goodness and grace
that will create. If you want nothing to do with love,
you will be given a reality free from love.

If, however, you crave light,
and you're drawn to truth,
and you're desperate for grace,
and you've come to the end of your plots and
schemes and you want a better path,
God will give you what you want.

If you have this sense that you've wandered far from
home,
and you want to return,
God is there,
standing there in the driveway,

arms open,
ready to invite you in.

These desires can start with the planting of an
infinitesimally small seed deep in our heart, or a
yearning for life to be better, or a gnawing sense that
we're missing out, or an awareness that beyond the
routine and grind of life there's something more, or
the quiet hunch that this isn't all there is. It often has
its birth in the most unexpected ways, arising out of
our need for something we know we do not have, for
someone that we know we are not.

And to that,
that impulse, craving, yearning, longing, desire—
God says yes.
Yes, there is water for that thirst,
food for that hunger,
light for that darkness,
relief for that burden.
If we want hell,
if we want heaven,
God says yes,
you can have what you want.
That's how love works.
It can't be forced, manipulated, or coerced.

It always leaves room for the other to decide.
And so, the one absolute we know for sure about the
fate of every single person in the world is that love
wins.

Love is what God is,
love is why Jesus came,
and love is why he continues to come,
year after year to person after person.

Love is why I've written this book, and
love is what I want to leave you with.

May you experience this vast,
expansive, infinite, indestructible love
that has been yours all along.
May you discover that this love is as wide
as the sky and as small as the cracks in
your heart no one else knows about.
And may you know,
deep in your bones,
that love wins.

RECOMMENDED READING

So, you want to go deeper and further? My hope is that the things I've been talking about in this book have created in you a desire to read and study and learn more. If that's the case, here are a number of books that have shaped me. Enjoy.

The Divine Conspiracy by Dallas Willard
This book is quite thick and takes a bit of work to get through, but it's worth it. The author talks about Jesus and the kind of life that Jesus teaches us to live. I read this in 1999, and it changed my life, giving me a whole new way to understand who Jesus is and what he came to do.

Christ the Lord: Out of Egypt and *Christ the Lord: The Road to Cana* by Anne Rice

Anne Rice became famous for her novels about vampires, but later she wrote these books about the life of Jesus after extensively researching what life was like in first century. Amazing.

The Return of the Prodigal Son by Henri J. M. Nouwen

This is actually a book about a man staring at a painting about a story that Jesus told. Incredible. This book did more to help me understand the love of God than anything else.

The Holy Longing by Ronald Rolheiser

The first chapter alone, where he writes about Princess Diana, Janis Joplin, and Mother Teresa, will be worth it.

Jesus, My Father, the CIA, and Me: A Memoir . . . of Sorts by Ian Morgan Cron

Seriously, you need to read this. And how great is that title?

AUTHOR Q & A

Why did you become a pastor?
Actually, I was in a band in college, and that's
what I thought I was going to do with my life. I
thought I was going to record and tour and write
songs and all that—but the band broke up in the
fall of my senior year of college and I had no plan
B. I was devastated. I had no idea what I was going
to do. And then gradually, over a period of time, I
started to think about being a pastor, and random
people I barely knew would stop me and say, "Have
you thought about being a pastor?" It was crazy.
And then I volunteered to preach a sermon at a
camp I was working at, and I was hooked. I realized
that creating things and sharing them with people

was my calling— it's what I feel like I was made
to do.

If you could give one piece of advice, what would it be?

Don't give up until you find work that you love.

What is the hardest thing you've ever had to do as a pastor?

Keep going. There are so many reasons to get cynical
and so many ways to lose your passion and get
burned out and forget why you're doing what you're
doing.

How do you get up and talk in front of so many people?

First, I always get butterflies. Even after twenty years
I still get nerves. That's what tells me that I'm really
living, that I'm in the game, that I'm throwing myself
into life. And second, hard work! I work and work
and prepare and go over it and over it for months
and months before I ever stand up there on the
stage. That way I know it so well that I'm free—I
can be spontaneous, I can react to the crowd, I can
appear as though I'm just having a chat with you
the audience—because I put so much work in to get

ready. It feels like giving a gift, like I get to do this and give this gift to these people and I'd rather be nowhere else.

What's the hardest ethical dilemma you've ever faced?

When I knew the truth about somebody and they were publicly saying things about me that weren't true, but defending myself or telling people what was really going on would have actually made things worse.

I can't shake the feeling that I've done bad things in my life. How do I get forgiven?

The compelling insistence of Jesus' message is that you've already been forgiven—that's the point of the cross. What Jesus invites you to do is trust that it's already true. That is the gospel, and it's a mind-blowing idea, huh? Now, that can be hard to trust, and what I've learned is that the best way to know it and feel it and experience it is to forgive somebody who's wronged you. That may seem impossible to do and it may take a long, long time and they may never have said that they're sorry and you may hate them, but if you forgive them you will tangibly feel the love of God because it's hard to give something you haven't already received.

Do you think people will start doing more bad things if they think they're going to get out of going to hell for those bad things?

No. That question raises the question: Is that the best God can do? Is the only motivation we have to do good that we don't want to be punished?

Do you have a favorite book?

Probably *The Divine Conspiracy*, or *The War of Art*, or *Lust for Life*, or John Robinson's *Honest to God*, or *Lamb: the Gospel According to Biff, Christ's Childhood Pal*.

Favorite band?

Midnight Oil or the Black Keys or Muse or the Killers or Bob Dylan.

Favorite TV Show?

Friday Night Lights, or *Game of Thrones*, or *The Wire*.

Favorite movie?

Ishtar, then *Chariots of Fire*, then *Comedian*.

If you could meet any living person, who would it be?

Eddie Izzard. Or Peter Garrett.

What's your idea of a perfect day?
Breakfast with my family, surfing, tacos for lunch,
surf some more, listen to a new record on my
turntable, give a talk somewhere, eat more tacos,
surf at sunset. . . .

What's the best piece of advice you've ever gotten?
"Your job is the relentless pursuit of who God made
you to be."

Do you have a favorite quote?
Yep. James Michener said: "The master in the art of
living makes little distinction between his work and
his play, his labor and his leisure, his mind and his
body, his information and his recreation, his love
and his religion. He hardly knows which is which. He
simply pursues his vision of excellence at whatever he
does, leaving others to decide whether he is working
or playing."

Do you have a favorite quote from the Bible?
"All things are yours."

**You're stranded on a desert island. Aside from a
Bible, what's the one thing you'd want with you?**
Why would I want a Bible? The first time it rained

it would be destroyed, and then I'd have nothing. I'd want a surfboard, preferably my 7'6" thruster, or maybe my 8' Swizzle, or the 9'6" Robert August, because that's where I meet God—out in the ocean, catching waves. The island has waves, right?

Aside from Jesus, who do you want to meet in heaven?
My grandfather Preston Bell.

Why did you leave your church?
Because it was an incredible ride to be there for twelve years and then it was time to do the next thing, and you have to know in life when one thing is coming to an end and the next thing is beginning, or you'll end up dying a slow death because you're holding on to the past instead of taking risks and leaps and trusting that there's something new just around the corner.

Where did the idea for the Nooma series come from?
My friends and I had a sense that there was some way to capture a sermon in visual form that had a cinematic feel to it, like a movie. But we hadn't seen anyone do it, so we had to try to figure it out. Which

was a ton of work, and lots of trial and error, and lots
of trusting our instincts.

How have you handled the criticism from some on *Love Wins*?

I have more joy than ever. When you're criticized, you
either fold and retreat and lose your passion or you
push through to the other side and find out that what
doesn't kill you makes you way, way stronger. Other
than that, you know how I respond? I wake up in the
morning and I make my kids breakfast and then I
take them to school and I sit down at my desk and I
absolutely throw myself into working on the next book.

Some of my friends are nonbelievers. Do I have an obligation to try to convert them?

It's better to think about it like a story. There is the
Jesus story, and you are doing all you can to live
out the Jesus story, and your friends are watching.
And like any great story, you talk about it in the
most natural ways because it's a part of you.
And you trust that what you find compelling and
fascinating in the Jesus story as it gets told in your
life will be compelling and fascinating to them and
they'll come to see it like you do. But that's out of
your control.

Are there dogs in heaven?

Why is it no one ever asks about cats? Or skunks? Or dolphins? Or ferrets? Or termites? Or Octopuses? . . . What is it about dogs? Aren't they the only animal that we have to clean up after? Doesn't that raise any red flags for anybody?

If you could add one more commandment to the Ten Commandments, what would it be?

Don't text while driving.